21 Side Hustles You Can Start Now

. . .

HENLEY GRIFFIN

CONTENTS

Introduction ... 7

Chapter 1
Side Hustle 101 ... 11

Chapter 2
Why Side Hustle? ... 15

Chapter 3
Money Matters ... 25

Chapter 4
Make Money Now ... 31

Learn More ... 64

Introduction

My first experience with doing side hustles started about eight years ago when I was attempting to become a problogger. As you might have guessed, that never really came to pass, though I did make a decent amount of side income from that project.

To this day, I still have lots of projects going on at once, so you could say that I have never really stopped side hustling. For me, it all started as a way to pay off student loan debt. Over time, my side hustles began to earn me more than my day job. So, when I was laid off from my last cubicle job, I did not have to get another one since my side hustles were making me enough money to pay my bills.

I know that not everyone wants to quit their day job and replace it with a side hustle or two. Some people just want to pay off debt like me and others might just want to make some cash for a big purchase or some travel. No matter what your reason for needing some side income, I have compiled more than 21 ideas that you can get started on today. That leaves you with no excuses when it comes to making extra money.

I deliberately chose side hustles that not only require no money to start, but that only require equipment or skills that I think most people already have access to at home or at the local library. This makes your side hustle almost risk free. It will only cost you the time that you need to put into it.

For a side hustle to be a big success, I think you need to focus on something that you enjoy. Otherwise, it is just another job. For that reason, I tried to include a variety of different ideas that would appeal to the most people.

This means that the list of side hustle ideas in this book is by no means complete. There are even plenty of other side hustles that you can start today with no investment needed. So, if you read this guide and don't come away with an actionable plan for making one of these ideas your new side hustle, I at least hope that it will inspire you enough to come up with something else that will work for you.

CHAPTER ONE

Side Hustle 101

Side Hustle Basics

If you're new to the concept of the side hustle, then you might be wondering what exactly it entails, how it differs from just another job, and how it can benefit you.

A side hustle is something that you do on the side, normally after you've done your regular day job or on weekends (sometimes both). The beauty of the side hustle is that it can be virtually anything that you think you can make money doing in your spare time.

Yes, if you already have a full-time job, then your side hustle is a second or part-time job. For that reason, side hustling is not for everyone. If you are the kind of person who likes to come home after work and veg out in front of the television, play video games or spend the night online, then you might not have what it takes to do a successful side hustle.

Make no mistake, a side hustle is work. And work means taking your free time and turning it into side hustle time. That means motivation is needed in order to do this thing.

Some side hustles are basically small businesses that require some equipment and start-up capital to begin. You won't find any of those in this book though as I've focused only on side hustles that most people can start on as soon as today. In most cases, you won't need to buy any additional equipment as you'll be able to use things that you already own. And, you will not need to spend a single cent to start hustling.

Side hustles offer a lot of benefits, which I'll go into detail on in the next chapter. The bottom line is that a side hustle can help you to make some positive changes in your life, both financial and career changes. Keep reading to learn why everyone should consider taking up a side hustle or two. Or, skip ahead to get ideas on zero dollar startup side hustles that you can start today.

CHAPTER TWO
Why Side Hustle?

Reasons To Side Hustle

The reasons for starting a side hustle vary from one person to the next and can range from things like the need to pay off some debt to a desire to make some extra money for a vacation in Cabo. Of course, you don't really need a reason to take on a side hustle to two, but it's something that I think everyone should consider.

In fact, I want to share some of the reasons that I think you should act on one, or more, of these side hustles. It does not have to be something that you want to do for the rest of your life, but you just might find that it lights up an entrepreneurial spark that changes the course of your life.

Let's look at some of the top reasons that you should start side hustling. Or, skip ahead to the next chapter if you're already convinced and ready to get some easy side hustle ideas.

You're The Boss

I've heard people who are not convinced of the awesomeness of side hustles complain that they are basically just a second job. Sure, that is technically true, except that most of the time when someone gets a second job it is just another position where they're working for the man. That's not true with side hustles.

When you choose a side hustle, you are the only person in charge (unless you deliberately choose a side hustle that has you working for someone else). That means no boss giving you busy work, busting your chops if you show up a few minutes late, or giving you grief when you don't want to work overtime.

Don't want to work your side hustle today? No problem! You don't even have to call anyone to let them know that you're taking the day off (unless your side hustle involves clients, that is). Want to take an extra long break and watch a few episodes of *Adventure Time*? Do it! There's no one to scold you for doing so.

Being your own boss is one of the best things about doing side hustles. You get to control everything from when you work to how much you get paid to how many hours you have to put in each day. It's a freedom that you don't get from a cubicle job and it feels pretty great.

That being said, there are some lucrative side hustles that you can do where you are working for someone else. You do still have a bit of freedom in this scenario since it is just a side income gig for you, and often you only have to work when you want.

Level Up Your Finances

Though many people start their own side hustles as a way to be their own boss, there are a lot of side hustlers out there who start out just looking to make some extra money.

Maybe you're in a dead end job with no chance of advancement. Maybe you've started listening to Dave Ramsey and want to start paying off your debt. Maybe you've got a big purchase coming up - vacation, Christmas presents, college tuition, house, engagement ring - and you need a way to finance it without going into debt.

The reason why you need to increase your cash flow really isn't important.

With a side hustle, or two, you can level up your finances and reach your financial goals on your own terms. Think of it as a way to supercharge your bank account.

Creating A Safety Net

Let's face it - anything can happen when it comes to your cubicle job and your finances. Just because you're a model employee and have been with the same company for too many years to count on one hand, doesn't mean that they'll employ you until you reach retirement age.

And just because you are financially fit right now doesn't mean that a financial disaster isn't right around the corner. You can't even use the excuse that you're healthy. I'm healthy, in fact, when I ended up in the emergency room earlier this year with appendicitis, the doctor remarked that I was in excellent health other than the inflamed appendix. Fortunately, I have health insurance, but if I had not then that bill, which totaled just over $30,000, would have been a definite financial disaster for me. Needless to say, such bills can bankrupt some people.

A side hustle helps prepare you for those "just in case" moments that can turn your finances upside down. Whether you want to call it a safety net, plan B or your fall-back plan, the point is that it's a great ace in the hole for those times when life gives you the middle finger.

Finally Do Something You Enjoy

It does not take much searching online to discover that the vast majority of people are just wasting their lives away doing things that they don't enjoy. Think about how many blog posts and books you've seen that help people "discover their passion" and such.

The hard truth is that if you intend to live your life working in a cubicle, then you're probably not going to be passionate about that.

Guess what? When you pick a side hustle, it can be something that you actually enjoy for a change. Who knows, you might even be so successful that you can quit that cubicle job and do the side hustle as a full time main hustle.

So, as you check out the 21 side hustle ideas that you can start today with out having to spend a single cent, do remember to look for something that actually excites you. And if you don't find something like that in my list, then use the 21 ideas as a sort of springboard to help you brainstorm up something that appeals to you as a viable side hustle.

Level Up Your Skills

In the immortal words of Napoleon Dynamite, "Girls only want boyfriends who have great skills." Whether you're trying to catch the eye of some hottie or just load up your resume with an impressive list of your own awesomeness, side hustles give you a legit opportunity to improve your skills.

For instance, maybe you want to start up a side hustle that offers web design services to local businesses. If you already know some HTML, then this gives you a chance to learn some more advanced skills like Photoshop for logos or even designing your own WordPress themes.

The cool thing about leveling up your skills is that as you gain new ones, you are able to expand your offerings. And this results in more income, either for new services or improved services.

It also gives you the ability to turn the side hustle into something much greater. Using the example above, as you become more of an expert in web design stuff, you could start a website on the topic that you use to funnel people to your paid course on Udemy or your book on Amazon. As your skills scale, so do your opportunities for income.

CHAPTER THREE

Money Matters

Getting Paid

Before you start a side hustle, it is a good idea to consider how you will get paid for it. For services that you offer online on your own, an online payment processor is probably the easiest way to conduct business. The most popular of these is PayPal.

If your side hustle has you working for another company, then it's probable that you will get paid via direct deposit or a regular paycheck.

If you are doing a side hustle in the real world instead of online, then you can accept multiple forms of payment. Obviously, cash is the easiest way to go. However, offering to accept credit cards might make your services more appealing. You can still use PayPal for this or use your iPhone or iPad and a card reader from Square for an inexpensive way to swipe customers credit cards in real-time.

You may also want to accept personal checks, but keep in mind that you will need to have your clients make out the check to your personal name. This applies even if you are promoting your side hustle as something like "Henley's Pet Walkers." Why? Because the only way that I could deposit a check made out to "Henley's Pet Walkers" would be if I opened up a business bank account for "Henley's Pet Walkers." And in order to do that, I would need a business license, which is not free.

"Getting Paid"

At some point in the future, you might want to get a business license if your side hustle is a big success or for liability reasons, but when you're just starting out it's not a necessity.

Taxes

According to the Internal Revenue Service website, once your side hustle earns you over $600, you are legally required to include the income on your Federal income tax return.

When you have to report your side hustle income, it also means that you are liable for taxes on that income. If you have a regular day job that withholds taxes and you normally get a tax refund, then you are likely fine and don't have to pay in anything extra. But if not, you may want to consider paying in quarterly self-employment taxes to avoid a penalty for not paying enough in during the tax year.

When you are doing your side hustle for a company, then you will probably get a 1099 form at the end of the year. When you get one of these, it means that the company has also sent a copy of it to the IRS. And, you should use this to claim the income on your tax return.

Please note that **I am not a qualified tax professional** and am only sharing information based on my experience doing side hustles. I suggest that you spend some time gathering information on the IRS website or chatting with a qualified tax professional about your personal tax situation to get some advice that will be of use to you.

CHAPTER FOUR

Make Money Now

21 Side Hustle Ideas

If you are ready to start trying your hand at some side hustles, I have compiled a collection of 21 different opportunities that might interest you.

Each of these side hustle ideas have the same thing in common - they require nothing for you to start. You do not need to spend a single cent to start earning from these side hustles right now.

For the side hustle ideas that you will find on the following pages, I have only included things that require equipment and/or skills that I think most people have, or have access to. For instance, if you come across an idea that requires a computer but you only have an iPad, remember that your local library most likely has computers that you can use for free. Likewise, if you see a side hustle that requires a specific type of computer program, remember that there are almost always free alternatives to the popular brands such as LibreOffice instead of Microsoft Office.

Some of these side hustles only offer the chance for a few hundred extra dollars per month while others can earn you thousands. I hope that you are inspired by the list and motivated enough to take action immediately. If you have any questions about any of these, feel free to contact me through my website.

Here are 21 one side hustle ideas for you to start on today.

Side Hustles 1 - 3

1. Online Video Courses

Monthly income potential: thousands

If you are an expert at something, then you can earn thousands of dollars per month just by creating video courses. The beauty of this is that you only have to create the course once and then it earns you some nice passive income in perpetuity.

Though you might think that you need some fancy equipment and a studio to film these courses, you couldn't be further from the truth. Sure, you can create video courses that you film with yourself in them. Plenty of people do just that. However, you can also create a slideshow in PowerPoint or record your computer screen with some screencast software and never actually appear in the video at all. You don't even need fancy audio software to record the sound.

Probably the biggest site for uploading your video couses is Udemy. There are a few other sites out there where you can earn from as well, but the big player here is Udemy and that is what I would focus on first. It doesn't cost you anything to upload the videos to Udemy and they allow you to put them on other sites at the same time.

You get to set the price for each course on Udemy. And you earn anywhere between 25% and 97% of the course list price. The amount that you earn depends on how the student found your course.

If you do a quick search online, then you will be able to find plenty of blog posts written by people who are crushing it with Udemy. I've seen instructors earning five figures per month with their courses. And plenty of Udemy instructors have quit their day jobs because they've earned so much.

Bare minimum of what you'll need to get started:

- Computer
- Powerpoint (or similar slide software) or screen recording software
- Audacity for audio recording
- Some type of microphone

Getting good audio is really important in order for Udemy to accept your video course. I know that not everyone has a USB microphone at home like me, so here are some no-budget options for you -

- Use your iPhone mic
- Use your wireless phone headset mic

If you don't have either of those things, then using the mic on your computer might work if you have a good, soundproof space to record your audio. My favorite way to get an audio clip without a lot of background noise is to go into a closet and cover my head with a thick blanket as I speak into the mic. It sounds really dorky, but it works surprisingly well. A voiceover actor gave me that tip a few years ago and I've been using it ever since.

If you are interested in making a serious go of this side hustle, I actually wrote an entire book on this subject that you might want to check out. You can find it listed here -- http://www.henleygriffin.com/books/

Or, do a web search for some tips on your own.

2. Brand Ambassador

Monthly income potential: hundreds

Have you ever gone to an event or conference and seen those people who stand out in the aisle trying to beckon you over to their booths or hadn you free stuff? Or what about those people in bars who are sharp dressed and trying to get you to taste a new liquor or beer? Or the people at the grocery store doing that in-store demonstration of the smoothie machine?

If you've seen those people, then you probably just thought that they were company employees working a little overtime. Wrong. Those are people working a side hustle as brand ambassadors.

Usually the main requirements for this gig are that you are friendly and outgoing. You don't have to look like an Abercrombie model to get work as a brand ambassador, unless you are trying to work for liquor companies and related brands who prefer to project a "beautiful people" image. For the most part though, your attractiveness level isn't really an issue. You just need to look presentable and be able to show up on time.

21 Side Hustles You Can Start Now

The pay rate for these gigs ranges between $15 and $20 per hour, depending on the city. And you normally work only one to two days. The hours that you work per day can range anywhere between two and 10 hours.

The work itself is really easy, but you do have to stand on your feet for those long hours. Most of the time, you are given a branded polo or t-shirt to wear at the event. And the rest of the dress code usually involves black or brown slacks with a white button-up shirt. And no, you can't wear your Converse All-Stars. Usually you have to wear nice dress shoes, but some companies are more casual and let you wear sneakers.

To find these side hustle jobs, you need to sign up with some event marketing companies like Victory Marketing and Attack! Marketing. You can do a search online for brand ambassador jobs and find plenty of companies to sign up with. You can also look on Craigslist for these jobs.

What you'll need to work this side hustle:

- brown or black slacks
- matching dress shoes
- white button-up shirt
- headshots
- resume

You don't have to go out and spend money on your headshots. Just get a friend to take a few closeups of you in your apartment against a solid color wall. If you've never seen a headshot before, just do a web search and take a look at some actor's headshots and aim for something similar.

3. Tutoring

Monthly income potential: hundreds to thousands

If you know your way around a subject or two and are good at teaching others, then you can make some pretty sweet cash by doing some tutoring. This is a side hustle that you can do online or in the real world. A quick web search will reveal plenty of sites where you can sign up to do online tutoring.

However, the big money is in real world tutoring. The amount that you can earn depends not only on your location, but your experience and the subject that you're tutoring a student in. Based on my research, the average starting rate is between $15 and $20 per hour, with plenty of tutors charging over $100 per hour.

To get those more lucrative hourly rates, you'll need to offer your services in affluent areas. Tutoring for standardized tests also commands you a higher rate; as does tutoring college students.

Before you go out and quote a rate of $100 per hour to people, see if you can find ads in your area from other tutors to get a grasp on the going rate for your locality. And remember, math and science tutors generally earn more than others.

Once you're ready to start taking on students, you need to let parents and students know what you're offering. This can be as easy as promoting yourself at the school or in the local community. Look at the places where people go who need a tutor and advertise yourself there. If you're good, then word of mouth will get you more students than you can handle.

The best part about this side hustle is that the only thing that you really need for it is knowledge of the subject.

Side Hustles 4 - 6

4. Trivia Night Host

Monthly income potential: hundreds to thousands

If you enjoy spending your evenings in bars or pubs and are the friendly and outgoing type, then hosting trivia nights can be a profitable side hustle for you.

Even if you don't spend much time in bars, you've probably heard of trivia nights. But if not, on these special nights there is a person (you) who is the sort of emcee for the night. That person asks all the trivia questions and is responsible for giving out the prizes to the winning teams. The event usually only lasts for a couple of hours.

There's actually two ways that you can approach this side hustle. If you want the no-budget route, then you need to sign up with a company that puts on trivia nights at bars across the nation. One such example is Trivia Tryst. When you take this path, you don't really need anything other than the ability to look presentable and be outgoing. The company provides you with everything else that you need.

But, if you can spend a little cash, then you can take this idea and effectively start your own trivia night company. Of course, you'd need to come up with the questions, possibly get yourself a microphone if you're targeting large bars, and approach companies for prizes. If you're interested in this route, I suggest that you first contract out with a company like Trivia Tryst to learn the in and outs of the business and then branch out on your own.

The amount of money that you make as a host really depends on the location that you happen to be in, with large cities offering higher rates. Plus, if you're in a big city, then you could do trivia night at a different bar several nights a week.

5. Pet Sitting

Monthly income potential: hundreds

Are you a pets person? If so, offering to babysit other people's critters is an easy way to make some money each month. There are a lot of opportunities for this side hustle since many pet owners do not want to leave their pets a kennel when they go on vacation.

Sometimes people even need their pet watched while they are at work during the day. I've even had friends who keep a pet in their apartment without the landlord knowing and need someone to take it during the day when the landlord is planning to come into the apartment.

While this gig often means keeping people's pets at your home, that is not always the case. When they're out of town, my parents pay someone to come to the house to give the dog food and water.

A quick way to line up clients for this side hustle is to identify some companies in your area that send their employees on a lot of business trips. There's a good chance that a chunk of those employees have pets that need taken care of while they're gone.

There's a pretty decent chance that you won't need to spend any money to start this side hustle. If you're going to people's homes to take care of their pets, then everything that you need will already be there. And if they're bringing the pets to you, then they're likely going to bring everything that they think it will need. The only expenses might be for things like water dishes or doggy gates in your home, if you don't already have those things.

And if this side hustle starts to become a big money maker for you, then you might want to consider getting some liability insurance in case something happens to any of the pets in your care.

6. Ride Share Drivers

Monthly income potential: hundreds

If you have your own vehicle and will come up clean on a background check, then turning your vehicle into a sort-of taxi is a good side hustle. In most major cities, you can sign up as a ride share driver with Uber or Lyft. Best of all, you don't have to pay anything to become a driver.

The process of getting the green light with each of these companies is slightly different. You may need to get your vehicle inspected by a staff member to ensure that it is clean and ready to transport people. You definitely will have to submit to a background check. And, some of the drivers are required to have commercial insurance.

Based on the drivers that I have talked to, you can average between $25 and $28 per hour during the surges, which are the hours when a lot of people need rides. People in large cities have more fare opportunities, and thus earn more than someone in a smaller city. For instance, drivers in Los Angeles are earning around $27 per hour during the surges right now, but those in the Inland Empire (Ontario and Riverside, California) are earning closer to $10 per hour during surges.

This side hustle might not be for everyone since you are picking up strangers, which could result in a dangerous situation. And since many of the surges are late nights, you could also end up with a drunk person vomiting in your car.

You also need to consider the wear and tear that this hustle puts on your car, not to mention the fuel expense. Granted, you can technically write off your mileage on your Federal income tax return as a legit expense.

Probably the most important thing to know when considering this side hustle is that the rideshare companies (Uber and Lyft) do not offer insurance to cover your vehicle. Instead, you are 100% liable for your vehicle. And most insurance companies are not covering accidents that happen when offering a ride share service. There is some pending legislation in California that might result in Uber being forced to insure riders, but that has not yet passed. You can learn more on this Reddit thread - http://www.reddit.com/r/uberdrivers/comments/2jg561/ can_someone_please_explain_the_insurance/

Based on what I've seen, the most successful people doing this side hustle live near airports and do most of their pick-ups during the day when they don't have to worry about drunk people messing up their rides. It can be an easy way to bank a couple hundred dollars a day in only a few hours at at time.

Side Hustles 7 - 9

7. Alterations

Monthly income potential: hundreds

I know it's not the sexiest of side hustles, but if you're good with a sewing machine then you can easily make some extra money by doing alterations in your community.

With this side hustle, you can offer your services to people who need things like pants altered. You can also branch out by offering your skills to the wardrobe department of local theaters. And if there are any dry cleaners in the area, you might be able to get them to recommend your services to their clients.

Obviously, this is not a side hustle that will make you enough money to pay all of your monthly bills. However, if you already have a sewing machine, then it is an easy way to make a few hundred extra bucks each month.

A good way to supercharge this side hustle is to advertise your alterations service heavily around the time of any school formals, such as prom. Some parents shop for their teen's formal attire at second-hand shops, which means the need for alterations is high during these periods.

8. Personal Assistant/ Errand Runner

Monthly income potential: hundreds

A lot of people hire other people to do small tasks and errands for them on a regular basis. This is something that can be done locally or online.

If you want to be a virtual assistant, then there are plenty of sites, like Odesk and Task Rabbit, that give you the ability to connect with people who need a VA. Your job duties can range from things like responding to emails to writing articles to gathering data to making phone calls. A lot of internet marketers hire a VA to help them build out websites and manage those sites. In fact, I regularly hire VAs to help me with my niche websites. And finding someone who can deliver work on-time is a real challenge. So, if you can offer that, you will stand out from everyone else.

If you prefer to get out of the house and be sociable, then offering your personal assistant services and/or errand running to the community is likely a better choice. The job duties are usually different than what you'd get as a virtual personal assistant, with most things falling into the errand running category. Things that you might do include organizing files, picking up mail, dropping off prescriptions and similar errands. In the real world, most of your clients will consists of either people running a small business or older people have trouble getting out of the house.

To start this side hustle, you should not need to buy anything. And your only expense will be fuel costs if you're offering this service in the local community.

9. eJuror

Monthly income potential: low hundreds

If you want a side hustle that brings in just a little extra money, like maybe enough to cover a car payment, then working as an eJuror is an easy way to do that.

This side hustle is exactly what it sounds like. You are part of an online jury. I know, it's not the most exciting side hustle, but it is easy money.

You can sign up to be an eJuror at eJury.com. The average time that you will spend on a case is only around 30 minutes. That's the good news. The sort of bad news is that you only make around $10 for your time. However, that's basically $20 an hour, right? So, if you can do enough of these in a month, then you end up with a few hundred bucks at best. The worst case scenario is that you make some easy money that only covers your cable bill or water bill.

You are paid for your time by PayPal, which is the only payment method that is offered at this time.

All you need for this side hustle is a computer, internet access and a PayPal account.

Side Hustles 10 - 12

10. Teach English As A Second Language

Monthly income potential: hundreds to thousands

If you've got a knack for teaching, then you might want to consider teaching English as a second language. While plenty of people do this side hustle in a classroom setting, you can actually do it online from the comfort of your home.

Just do a quick web search for "teach English online" and you'll find plenty of sites that hook up English teachers with students. You can also advertise your services in expat and language forums so that you can pick up some clients on your own; or post an ad on sites like Odesk for more reach.

You should consider specializing so that you can make even more money from this side hustle. I have a friend, who is a native French speaker, that makes her living teaching business English to companies. She does some of the teaching in person at company offices and others online via Skype-type sessions. She's earned enough to buy a house and support herself.

For even more earning opportunities, you can video record some of your lessons and offer them as online courses.

If you do not already have a headset and a web cam, then you may need to get those for the online teaching. But you don't need anything extra to offer classroom courses.

11. Writing

Monthly income potential: hundreds to thousands

If you are decent at writing, then you can make a considerable side hustle income from that skill. There are a variety of different sites that you sign up with as a freelance writer, from Odesk to Textbroker to Writer Access. And there is just as much variety when it comes to what you can get paid to write.

You might get paid to write blog posts, a video script, product descriptions, ebooks, press releases, directory listing details, articles and more. The better your writing, the higher your rate of pay. And if you can specialize, such as WordPress articles or copywriting, then you can earn even more than as a generalist.

The only thing that you need for this side hustle is access to a computer and the internet.

If this sounds like an appealing side hustle, then you can do a web search to identify places to hock your talent, or check out my guide on this subject - Make Money From Home As A Freelance Writer (Cubicle Freedom Series). You can find it listed here -- http://www.henleygriffin.com/books/

Freelance writing is a side hustle that I've done for many years as my undergrad degrees are in English and Journalism. I've had years where I earned enough for a good lifestyle, with plenty of travel, doing nothing but freelance writing. It's one of my favorite side hustles because you can do it from anywhere in the world.

Remember, you can also just contact websites that have a "Write for Us" page and attempt to get work that way. You can often find writing gigs that pay around $50 starting out for blog posts with this method.

12. Pet Taxi

Monthly income potential: hundreds

If you enjoy pets and have your own vehicle, then operating a pet taxi side hustle is an easy way to make some extra money on your own time.

With this type of service, you will do things like pick up pets and take them to appointments at the vet or the groomers, or just bring them back home after these types of appointments. It's not really a lot of work at all, with the only real expense being fuel costs.

I recently heard about a guy who managed to get all the local pet crematoriums to give out his pet taxi details. This enabled him to supercharge his side hustle by getting a lot more clients. Granted, he was transporting mostly dead animals at that point, but he was making good money doing it.

Since most pet owners already own pet carriers, it's unlikely that you'll have to spend anything to start this side hustle. Once you make a little money though, you might want to consider getting a few pet carriers of your own for clients who don't have them.

Side Hustles 13 - 15

13. Junk Specialist

Monthly income potential: hundreds to thousands

Do you have a truck and don't mind a bit of manual labor? If so, you can make a healthy side income helping people clean out their garages and hauling away their unwanted junk.

The easiest way to find people that need this service is just to look on Craigslist. You can also advertise your junk specialist service on Craigslist and other local sites and papers.

The interesting thing about this side hustle is that it has the opportunity to make you a lot more money on top of the cleaning and junk hauling. In fact, I know of a few people that have made a tidy sum selling the junk that they hauled away from people's houses. Whether people don't know what they've got or just don't care, it puts you in the perfect place to profit from other people's junk without spending a cent.

Obviously, you need to have a pick-up truck for this side hustle. And your only real expense is fuel costs for your truck.

One thing to keep in mind is that some people may try to get you to take away junk that you cannot legally discard. So, before you accept any jobs, inquire as to the type of junk that the potential client wants to get rid of before you agree to take the job.

14. Elderly Sitter

Monthly income potential: hundreds

The elder care market is one that is growing rapidly since we have such a large aging population in the United States. As a result, that leaves a lot of families in need of someone to basically keep older adults company during the day.

Do not confuse this gig with home hospice care. Your job is to be with the elderly client during the day when family members are at work. Duties typically include things like making sure that medicine gets taken, making meals and just keeping the older client safe and out of trouble. Often families need someone to do this when they have an older family member who is too healthy to go into a nursing home or have a home nurse or hospice worker, but may be forgetful or not able to cook for themselves.

This is a side hustle that is perfect for parents with small children. Why? Because most of the elderly clients don't mind that you bring the child with you while you are sitting with them during the day.

Most of the time, this side hustle is during the day and only Monday through Friday. Of course, that can vary from one client to the next.

This is something that you can register to do with an agency or go out on your own. The average price for this is around $50 per day, which isn't a lot of money. Higher rates are more common in cities and more affluent areas. It's difficult to charge a lot for this side hustle service since often the families who need it are cash-strapped due to medical bills. Plus, do you really want to do something as karmically bad as price gouging the elderly?

All that you'll need for this side hustle is a vehicle to get you to the client's home. However, if you sign up through an agency, then expect to have to go through a background check first.

Keep in mind that if you have any references, even from baby-sitting, it will go a long way in helping you to secure clients.

15. Fiverr

Monthly income potential: hundreds to thousands

If this isn't the first time that you've looked for side hustle ideas, then you've likely already discovered the website Fiverr. This nice thing about this site is that virtually anyone can find something that they can offer for sale on the site.

Before you get started, know that you only end up pocketing $4 from each $5 sale as the site takes a 20% cut. If you're wondering how you can end up making thousands of dollars a month at such rates, the secret is in the upsell, which are called additions on the site.

Once you have sold your gig to a few people and gotten positive reviews, your level on the site increases. When that happens, you suddenly have the ability to include add-on services on each gig that you offer on the site. It's common to see things like 24-hour delivery offered for an extra fee. Some enterprising people have even made it so that you get nothing for your $5 unless you buy their $100 add-on. You can see an example of what these add-ons look like in action with this seller - https://www.fiverr.com/crorkservice

The best way to maximize your hourly rate on Fiverr is to identify things that you can do in about 15 minutes or less. That gives you a decent hourly rate of around $16 per hour. Of course, once you can include the add-ons in your listings, you have the ability to increase that hourly rate even more.

Another way to increase the money that you earn from this side hustle is to create multiple gigs on the site. You are allowed to have up to 20 gigs at one time.

Fiverr pays you by PayPal and they do not cover the money transfer fee. For that reason, it is a good idea to let some of your income build up in your account before you request to be paid.

Side Hustles 16 -18

16. Renting Out Spare Rooms

Monthly income potential: hundreds to thousands

This is probably another side hustle that you've heard of before, but it is such a profitable one that I included it in this list. Though you can rent out spare rooms on sites like Craigslist, the most profitable way to do so is through Airbnb.

Through that site, you are able to rent out the space on a nightly basis as if your home is a hotel. Obviously, this is something that works best if you are in a city and not the suburbs.

Unfortunately, this side hustle is not for everyone. In fact, some cities and states have made it illegal for you to rent out spare rooms on sites like Airbnb. So, before you decide that this is how you will make some extra money on the side, check out and see what the laws are in your area. And if you are currently renting your home, then you definitely might get in trouble for renting out a room like this if your rental lease prohibits it.

I also want to mention that this is not a risk-free endeavor. In the past, some people using Airbnb have seen their apartments trashed by renters. And unfortunately, Airbnb doesn't seem to have a good system in place for when this happens.

Additionally, if someone gets hurt while staying in your place, then you could end up in a sticky legal situation in terms of liability issues.

That being said, all it takes is a quick web search to find plenty of people making thousands of dollars per month just by renting out a spare room on Airbnb. And the amount that you can earn in a month depends on how much you can charge per night for your area and how many nights you want to rent out the space each month.

17. Translation Services

Monthly income potential: hundreds to thousands

If you can speak, read and write in another language, then you can make some money utilizing those skills by offering translation services. While you'll probably attract some high school and college students who want you to do their foreign language home work, you can also sell this service to business people, website owners, authors and other content creators.

I know of several authors who pay people on Odesk to translate their books into other languages. While some of these books are short non-fiction titles, others are works of fiction over 300 pages. As you can see, a serious amount of money can be made in this side hustle.

To get started, you could offer a small version of this side hustle for sale on Fiverr. For instance, you could create a gig offering to translate 300 words of text.

For a great income potential, sign up on freelancer marketplaces like Odesk so that it's easy for clients to find you. Or, do a web search for specialized sites where you can meet clients in need of translation services.

Once you start earning money from this side hustle, spend a little money creating a website where you can offer this service to anyone who lands on your site.

Depending on how much work you want to take on, this is a side hustle that can easily earn enough money to turn into a full-time main hustle that can replace your day job.

And if you don't mind teaching, you could combine this service with the teaching English as a second language side hustle and make even more side income.

18. Tax Preparation

Monthly income potential: hundreds

Tax preparation is one of those things that seems to really intimidate a lot of people. The funny thing about it is that most people only have one job that gives them a W-2 at the end of the year, and they don't have any odd tax situations going on. Basically, just an easy, straight-forward return.

Do they do that tax return on their own?

Most of the time, no, at least not in my experience. I know people who have held the exact same job and been a single non-home owner for the past 15 years and they still pay some minimum wage temporary employee at H&R Block around $200 to file their tax return.

That money could be yours, my friend.

To get an idea of what people are paying to get their taxes done, check out this article on About.com -- http://taxes.about.com/od/findataxpreparer/a/prices.htm

With an average cost of close to $200, you could charge $100 and make a decent amount of money for your time AND save the other person almost $100 in the process.

Before you jump on this side hustle, keep in mind that tax season is limited, which means that you only have a chance to make money from this side hustle during the first quarter of each year. Also keep in mind that as the tax preparer, you have to sign each tax return that you prepare. This means that if the Internal Revenue Service finds a problem, then it's your ass on the line for it. That being said, it's unlikely that you'll have any problems, but you should be aware of the possible situation. I've been helping people file their tax returns for about 10 years now and never had any issue.

To do this side hustle, you don't even need any type of certification or training. The easiest way to do it is to just use an online taxing filing site, like Turbo Tax. Sure, there is a fee to use a site like this for some returns, but you should still end up with enough money to cover your time at a decent hourly rate. Just remember to charge more for doing business taxes or those of self-employed people who will have a lot of things to write-off.

Side Hustles 19 - 21

19. Local Tour Guide

Monthly income potential: hundreds

Ever visit a city and see a walking tour made up of a bunch of tourists and a man or woman leading the pack of them? That local tour guide just might be working a pretty cool side hustle.

If you live in an area that gets some tourists, then you can start earning some side money by offering walking tours of the area. Often the way that these work is that interested tourists meet at a specified location at a certain time of day. Then, you show up and lead them to all the significant sights.

Sometimes these walking tours are free and the guide strongly encourages participants to tip at the end of the tour. Other times there is a small fee...and tips are still strongly encouraged at the end of the tour. In my experience, nightly ghost tours seem to be the ones that have the most success with charging a walking tour fee.

Before you go stock up on facts about your city, first check with your local government to see if you need a license to conduct the tours. If so, then this won't be a free side hustle. And unfortunately, some localities won't let you offer the tours without being licensed. But for those localities who don't require licensing, all you need is some facts and a place to advertise your walking tours.

You can find plenty of places online to advertise for free. You can even create a free website to promote your walk; though I do recommend getting a real domain name once you can afford it so that you don't look like an amateur.

Once you've made some money, consider getting some flyers printed up to place in local businesses as a way to be seen by more tourists. It will be a good investment of your earnings as it should drive you more business.

20. Search Engine Evaluator

Monthly income potential: thousands

This is one of my very favorite side hustles because you can easily make a full-time income from it while working from home. I have been doing this as a side hustle for about three years now and I average around $22,000 per year with this side hustle.

The best thing about it is that the work is super easy and I can often do it while watching television or movies. Basically, when my brain can't handle any complex tasks, I do a bit of this side hustle for the easy money.

Of course, you don't have to strive for more than a thousand dollars a month from this gig as you can easily make it a very part-time one.

Pay is by direct deposit and happens about 25 days after the end of the month.

A few different companies offer this gig. The main two are Lionbridge and Leapforce. A cool thing about this side hustle is that it's open to people outside of the United States.

Before getting excited about this potential side hustle, know that you do have to take a test in order to get hired. The test is just simulations of the type of tasks that you have to do in the actual job. Fail the test and you lose your chance at the gig; but you can apply at one of the other companies if that happens.

All you need to do this side hustle is a computer with the Chrome web browser (Firefox used to be required but no more) and an internet connection.

Note that no two people can share the same IP address, which means that if you and your girlfriend both want to do this, then you can't apply or work from the same IP address. Ever.

Of course, this is easily overcome with one of those MiFi internet devices that you can buy from your local cell phone shop. One of you could use the home internet connection while the other uses the MiFi device. And I have no confirmation of this, but I suspect that you can't share a mailing address either, so use a relative's or get a post office box.

If you want some in-depth information on this side hustle, I actually wrote an entire book on this subject that you might want to check out. You can find it listed here -- http://www.henleygriffin.com/books/. It should answer any questions that you have about the gig.

21. Movie or TV Extra

Monthly income potential: hundreds

With so many television shows and movies filming in random areas of the United States and Canada, you no longer have to live in Los Angeles or New York to get work as an extra. In fact, there are currently things filming in places like Wilmington, North Carolina; New Orleans, Louisiana; Charlotte, North Carolina; Nashville, Tennessee, Portland, Oregon; and Vancouver, Canada (just to name a few).

The beauty of extra work is that it requires no real skills. You just need to be able to show up on time and do what they tell you to. Your whole job for the day could be to just walk by an elevator when you are told to do so. Or maybe you're supposed to be sitting at a desk looking like you're working. It's really that easy.

The cool thing about extra work is that you get the chance to get close to celebrities. Some extras even get to take photos with them while they're on set. Another cool thing is that you get to eat for free while on set.

All you need to get started working as an extra is a headshot and resume. Don't worry if you've never done any acting work because you won't be speaking. You'll just be what is called a background player. Your job is to blend in to the scene and not really be noticed.

Unless you happen to be a member of the Screen Actors Guild (SAG), the base pay rate for your extra work is around $55 per day for up to 8 hours of work. If you work longer than eight hours, then you can earn more money. And if you are a member of SAG, then the base rate is around $115 per day.

Finding the casting calls for extra work isn't all the difficult, but you do sometimes need to check regularly for new casting calls. One way to find them is to check the website for your state's film commission. This is usually where movies that are filming in the state post their casting calls.

You'll also want to seek out any casting companies in your area and sign up with them. They normally get an early lead on any projects casting extras in the area. And the Backstage website is another great place to look. Check it out here - http://www.backstage.com/casting/open-casting-calls/extras-casting/

You will need a couple of headshots to submit to casting companies. There's no need to pay for these as a friend, a good digital camera and a solid color wall are all you need. Check out the headshots of some actors online and try to take something similar.

Bonus! More Ideas!

If you want a few more ideas of things that you can do for a side hustle without spending any money up front, then I have a few more things to share with you. While many of these will only bring in a small amount of side money, there are a few that can make you a decent chunk of cash each month.

- Sign up with market research companies for paid focus groups
- Look for medical studies in your city as some of these pay thousand of dollars
- Offer to clean people's houses
- Spend some time creating content on Web 2.0 sites, like Hubpages, where you can earn some revenue share money
- Check out Mturk and see if you can make a little cash while you're watching television or in other down time
- Help people with their computer problems
- Teach people (the older generation) how to use new technology
- Sell your photos on stock photo websites
- Babysit the neighborhood kids after school until their parents get home from work

Learn More

Enjoy this book? Please let others readers know by leaving a review for it online. Then, let me know so that I can thank you!

I hope that you found value in this book and are able to choose a good side hustle that you can start working on today. If you have any questions, you can reach me through the contact form on my website.

And if you are looking for a side hustle to replace your current job, then you might be interested in my Cubicle Freedom Series. Each book in the series gives an in-depth look at a side hustle that has the ability to replace your day job. You can find out more about this series on the next page.

You May Also Be Interested In...

The Cubicle Freedom Series focuses on ways that you can make real money working online from home. All of the opportunities found in the books of the series have been tried out personally by the author.

The aim of this series is to find jobs that enable you to leave that terrible cubicle job and experience the freedom of working from home - or anywhere else in the world that you may like!

"Learn More"

Most of the books in the series give you a single online job that can replace your cubicle job income. Sometimes, though, jobs are listed that only offer enough income to equal that of a part-time job. In such instances, you can pair one of those jobs with another one from the series and comfortably earn enough in your pajamas to pay all of your family's bills.

For more information on the Cubicle Freedom Series, visit the official website at: http://www.cubiclefreedomseries.com/

To be notified of future releases in this series, go sign up for the notification list at: http://eepurl.com/BZlVT or http://www.cubiclefreedomseries.com/books/

About The Author

Henley Griffin has been earning a full-time income online since late 2008/early 2009. Currently, the author earns around $7,000 per month online while averaging a work schedule that consists of three weeks of work followed by three weeks of traveling.

After seeing so many friends and family members lose jobs in the recession, Henley has been helping to teach people how to break free from traditional employment and enjoy the fruits of working online at home.

You can find more information on the author at Henley's personal website: http://www.henleygriffin.com/

Other books by Henley include:

Make Money From Home As A Google Rater (Cubicle Freedom Series)
Make Money From Home Teaching Online Video Courses (Cubicle Freedom Series)
Make Money From Home As A Freelance Writer (Cubicle Freedom Series)
Beginners Guide To Building A Private Blog Network

21 Side Hustles You Can Start Now

###